Millionaire Habits How to think, act and live like the rich

Elias saba

DEDICATION

ITo all those who dream of achieving success

To those who are willing to work hard and never give up

To those who believe that everything is possible

This book is for you

I hope it inspires you to develop millionaire habits and achieve your most ambitious goals.

Never stop dreaming!

With affection,

Elias saba

CONTENTS

ACKNOWLEDGMENTS

This book would not have been possible without the help and support of many people.
First of all, I would like to thank my family for their unconditional love and constant support. To my partner for his patience and understanding during the long hours I spent writing this book. To my children for being my source of inspiration and motivation.
I would also like to thank my friends and colleagues for their valuable advice and suggestions. To my mentors for guiding me on my path to success. To all those who have believed in me and my potential.
In a special way, I would like to thank:
The people who gave me invaluable help in researching and editing the book.
Those who gave me financial support and believed in this project from the beginning.
Those who gave me advice on marketing and promotion.
The artist who designed the book cover.
To all of them, my sincere thanks.
I would also like to thank the readers who have purchased this book. Your interest and support motivate me to continue writing and sharing my knowledge with the world.
I hope this book will help you achieve your dreams and live a full and meaningful life.
Thank you for reading!

Chapter 1: The millionaire mentality

What sets millionaires apart from other people? It's not just their money, but their mindset. Millionaires have a unique mindset that enables them to achieve success and abundance.

In this chapter, you will discover the key characteristics of the millionaire mindset and how you can develop them to achieve your own goals.

Beliefs about money:

Millionaires have positive beliefs about money. They believe that money is a good thing and that it is possible to earn it honestly. They also believe that they deserve to be rich and that they can achieve their financial goals.

2. Attitude toward risk:

Millionaires are not afraid to take risks. They are willing to step out of their comfort zone and try new things. They know that failure is part of the road to success and that you should not give up at the first hurdles.

3. Discipline and focus:

Millionaires are disciplined and focused people. They have clear goals and know how to achieve them. They are not easily distracted and are able to stay focused on their objectives.

4. Perseverance:

Millionaires are persevering. They do not give up easily in the face of challenges. They know that success takes time and effort, and they are willing to work hard to achieve their goals.

5. Abundance mentality:

Millionaires have an abundance mentality. They believe that there is enough money for everyone and that it is not necessary to compete with others to achieve success.

Exercises:
* Identify your limiting beliefs about money.
* Develop an abundance mindset.
* Visualize your financial success.

Chapter 2: Daily Habits for Success

Millionaires not only have a different mindset, but they also have different habits. These habits allow them to be more productive, efficient and successful in all areas of their lives.
In this chapter, you'll discover the most important daily habits that millionaires share and how you can incorporate them into your own routine to achieve your goals.

1. Wake up early:
Millionaires tend to wake up early. This gives them time to get their most important activities done before the day begins.

2. Exercise:
Regular exercise is essential for physical and mental health. Millionaires know that exercise helps them have more energy, concentrate better and be more productive.

3. Meditate or practice mindfulness:
Meditation and mindfulness are practices that help reduce stress, increase mental clarity and improve concentration. Millennials use these practices to improve their well-being and performance.

4. Read:
Millennials are avid readers. They know that reading helps them learn new things, broaden their view of the world and develop new ideas.

5. Plan the day:
Millionaires plan their day in advance. This allows them to make the most of their time and achieve their goals more efficiently.

6. Set goals:
Millionaires have clear and defined goals. They know what they want to achieve and have a plan to get there.

7. Visualize success:
Millionaires visualize their success on a regular basis. This helps them stay motivated and focused.

8. Surround yourself with positive people: Millionaires know that the company one keeps is important. They surround themselves with positive people who support them and help them achieve their goals.

9. Help others:
Millionaires are generous with their time and money. They know that helping others is a way to give back to the community and make the world a better place.

10. Get enough sleep:
Sleep is essential for physical and mental health. Millennials know that getting enough sleep helps them be more productive and efficient.

How do you incorporate these habits into your

own routine?

Start with one or two habits and gradually incorporate the others.

Be consistent and don't give up if you don't see immediate results.

Create a tracking system to help you stay motivated.

Remember that habits are formed with time and effort. If you are willing to work at it, you can develop the daily habits that will lead to success.

Exercises:
* Create a powerful morning routine.
* Set SMART goals and create an action plan.
* Develop discipline and perseverance.

Chapter 3: The Importance of Physical and Mental Health

Physical and mental health are two fundamental pillars of success. Millionaires know that taking care of their body and mind is essential to achieving their goals.
In this chapter, you'll discover why physical and mental health is so important to success and how you can improve it.

Importance of physical health:

Increased energy: When you're physically healthy, you have more energy to meet the challenges of everyday life.

Better concentration: Regular physical activity improves concentration and memory.

Greater productivity: Physically healthy people are more productive at work and in study.

Better mood: Regular exercise helps reduce stress and anxiety, and improves mood.

Lower risk of disease: Taking care of your body helps you prevent chronic diseases such as diabetes, high blood pressure and heart disease.
Importance of mental health:

Better decision-making ability: When you are mentally healthy, you can make better decisions and solve problems more effectively.

Greater resilience: Mental health helps you cope with life's setbacks and difficulties.

Better relationships: Mentally healthy people have better relationships with others.

Greater satisfaction with life: Mental health helps you enjoy life and feel fulfilled.

How to improve your physical and mental health?

Healthy eating: Eat a diet rich in fruits, vegetables, whole grains and lean proteins.

Regular physical activity: Get at least 30 minutes of moderate-intensity exercise most days of the week.

Get enough sleep: Get 7 to 8 hours of sleep each night.

Manage stress: Practice relaxation techniques such as meditation or yoga.

Connect with others: Spend time with loved ones and participate in social activities.

Remember that physical and mental health are investments that will pay off in the long run.

Long term. If you take care of your body and mind, you will be better prepared to achieve your goals and live a full and meaningful life.

Exercise:

* Implement a regular exercise routine.

* Adopt a healthy, balanced diet.

* Practice mindfulness and meditation techniques.

Chapter 4: How to invest your money wisely

Millionaires know that investing their money is one of the best ways to make it grow. Not only do they work hard to make money, but they also work hard to make their money work for them. In this chapter, you'll discover the basics of smart investing and how you can start investing your money effectively.

1. Define your goals:
Before you start investing, it's important to define your goals. Do you want to save for retirement? Buy a home? Start a business? Your goals will help you determine what type of investments are right for you.

2. Do your research before you invest:
Don't invest in anything you don't understand. Do your research before investing in any asset, and make sure you understand the risks and rewards involved.

3. Diversify your portfolio:
Don't put all your eggs in one basket. Diversify your portfolio by investing in different types of assets, such as stocks, bonds, real estate and cash.

4. Invest for the long term:
Long-term investments are the best way to grow your money significantly. Don't try to get rich

quick with speculative investments.

5. Reinvest your profits:
Reusing your earnings will help you grow your money even faster.

6. Be patient:
Investing is a long-term game. Don't expect to get rich overnight. Be patient and disciplined, and over time your investments will pay off.

How to start investing?
Open a brokerage account.
Research different types of investments.
Choose an investment strategy that fits your goals and risk tolerance.

Start investing with small amounts.
Monitor your investments and adjust your strategy as needed.

Remember that investing is a continuous learning process. The more you learn, the better investment decisions you will make.

Exercises:
* Learn the basics of investing.
* Define your investor profile.
* Develop a long-term investment strategy.

Chapter 5: Living a Full and Meaningful Life

Millionaires know that success is not just about money. It's about living a full and meaningful life.

In this chapter, you'll discover how you can live a fuller, more meaningful life, regardless of your income level.

1. Find your passion:
What are you passionate about, what makes you feel alive? Find your passion and devote time to it.

2. Set meaningful goals:
What do you want to achieve in life? Set goals that are important to you and work to achieve them.

3. Help others:
Helping others is one of the best ways to find satisfaction in life. Find a cause you are passionate about and get involved.

4. Cultivate your relationships:
Relationships are one of the most important things in life. Invest time in cultivating relationships with your loved ones.

5. Enjoy the present:
Don't miss the present by worrying about the past or the future. Enjoy every moment and live

to the fullest.

6. Be grateful:

Be grateful for the good things in your life, both big and small. Gratitude will help you be happier and more positive.

7. Be true to yourself:

Don't try to be someone you are not. Be true to yourself and live your life according to your own values.

Remember that life is a gift. Make the most of every moment and live a full and meaningful life.

Exercises:

* Identify your values and priorities.
* Develop positive relationships with the people around you.
* Be grateful for what you have and give to others.

Additional practical exercises:

* Keep a journal to track your habits.
* Join a mastermind group or find a mentor.
* Participate in workshops and seminars on personal and financial development.
* Read books and articles on topics that interest you.

Positive affirmations:

* Write 10 positive affirmations about your wealth and success. Repeat them daily with conviction.

* Example: "I am a money magnet. I attract wealth into my life with ease.

2. Visualization:

* Spend 10 minutes a day visualizing yourself living the life you desire. Imagine what your house, your car, your lifestyle would be like.
* The more vivid your visualization is, the more likely you are to turn it into reality.

SMART Goals:

* Set specific, measurable, achievable, relevant and time-bound goals.
* Break your big goals into smaller, more manageable steps.
* Celebrate each achievement, no matter how small.

4. Action plan:

* Create a detailed action plan to achieve your financial goals.
* Define what actions you need to take each day, week and month.
* Be disciplined and consistent in the execution of your plan.

5. Track your habits:

* Track your financial habits for one week.
* Identify the habits that are helping you reach your goals and those that are holding you back.
* Implement changes to improve your habits

and create a richer life.

6. Networking:

* Surround yourself with positive and successful people who inspire you.
* Attend events and groups where you can meet people with similar interests.
* Build strong relationships that will benefit you on your path to wealth.

7. Inspirational reading:

* Read books and articles on financial success and personal development.
* Surround yourself with information that motivates you and helps you grow.
* Spend at least 30 minutes a day reading.

8. Gratitude:

* Practice gratitude for the good things you have in your life.
* Write in a gratitude journal and write down 3 things you are grateful for each day.
* Gratitude will help you maintain a positive attitude and attract more wealth into your life.

9. Help others:

* Look for opportunities to help others without expecting anything in return.
* Altruism will open new doors and connect you with people who can help you reach your goals.

* Sharing your success with others will make you feel good about yourself.

10. Stay motivated:

* Remember your why and keep your motivation high.
* Visualize the benefits of achieving your goals.
* Celebrate your achievements and don't give up in the face of obstacles.

Remember: success is not achieved overnight. It requires discipline, effort and persistence. Implement these exercises in your daily life and you will see long-term results.

11. Invest in your financial education:

Learn about personal finance, investing and wealth building.
There are many resources available online, in libraries and in specialized courses.
The more knowledge you have, the better decisions you can make with your money.

12. Take care of your health:

Your health is your greatest wealth. Make sure you get enough sleep, eat healthy and exercise regularly.
A healthy lifestyle will give you the energy and mental clarity you need to achieve your goals.

13. Be patient:

Success doesn't happen overnight. Be patient and stay focused on your goals.
There will be difficult times, but if you persevere, you will eventually achieve your dreams.

14. Enjoy the journey:

Don't obsess about the final destination. Enjoy the process of learning and growing.
Life is too short not to enjoy it. Find the balance between working hard and living a full life.

Remember that success is not a destination, but a journey. It takes effort, dedication and time to develop millionaire habits. However, if you are willing to work hard and never give up, you can achieve your dreams and live a full and meaningful life.

ABOUT THE AUTHOR

Elias Saba is a Lawyer and Naturopathic Doctor passionate about healthy living, nutrition and both physical and mental health. He considers habits and organization as one of the keys to a successful life, along with discipline and health.

In his book Millionaire Habits: How to Think, Act and Live Like the Rich, Elias shares his experience and knowledge to help readers develop habits that lead to a fuller and more abundant life.

His goal is to reach millions of people and help them achieve their dreams and goals. He wants each person who reads this book to be inspired to take action, organize their life and develop the habits that will allow them to achieve success in all aspects of their life.

He believes that we all have the potential to achieve great things, we just need the right tools and motivation. This book will give you both. Whether you want to improve your health, increase your income or simply live a happier and more organized life, this book will help you achieve it.

He invites you to join him on this journey to a better life.

Together we can achieve our dreams!

Conclusion

Millionaire Habits: How to Think, Act and Live Like the Rich has given you the tools and knowledge you need to achieve success in all areas of your life.

Remember that success is not just about money. It's about living a full and meaningful life.

Apply the advice in this book in your daily life and you will see how you can improve your physical and mental health, increase your wealth, build stronger relationships and live a happier, more fulfilling life.

The road to success is not easy, but with effort, dedication and the right attitude, you can achieve anything you set your mind to.

Start living the life you've always dreamed of today!

Here are some additional tips to help you reach your goals:

Surround yourself with positive, successful people.

Read books and articles on personal development.

Attend seminars and workshops on success.

Invest in your education and personal development.

Take action and never give up.

I wish you much success on your way to the top!